Gates of Guilford

selected poems & photographs

Lanzi W. Butler

Edited by Eugene Healy

❧

MBT
Guilford, Connecticut

ISBN 0-9768419-0-8
Copyright ©2005 by L.W. Butler

Although the photographs in this book were taken from the public domain in and around the historic areas of Guilford, CT., the author would like to ask the readers to respect the privacy of the home owners.

The definitions of these poetry forms can be found in your local libraries or on the internet.

———————————

Permissions and requests should be mailed to:

MBT
P.O. Box 215
Guilford, CT. 06437

Edited by Eugene Healy
Photograph on page 15, cover and book design by Geri Mancini

Library of Congress Control Number: 2005925142

First edition - 2005
Printed in the United States of America by:
Royal Printing Service, Guilford, CT.

Special thanks to my sister Abby for her "radiant reflections", to Cris & John for their generous support and to my parents who gave me endless guidance throughout this entire project.

To CEM and Cooper.

Contents

Introduction

"Crocidile"

Chomp Chomp in the
River
On the land
Chomp more
In the Nile
Down the Nile
In the Nile again
Lie in the sun
Electrick Crocs.

My interest in poetry began in Mrs. M's first grade class. For me, school was an interruption to my boundless world of play and fantasy. But somehow, writing words sideways and in different shapes was a new and interesting game, so I listened. At the age of six, my first attempt at poetry was in the form of an *acrostic* poem — my impressions of a crocodile. At the time, this was the only form of poetry I knew and even today it is one of the most popular styles of poetry for children to write. Little did I realize that my misspelling of "crocidile" and the complete irrelevance to "Electrick" in the last line of my poem, became a cornerstone for a poet under construction.

Throughout elementary school, my parents encouraged my poetry. Soon, I became interested in other forms and styles, most notably, *haiku*. When I encountered the 5-7-5 haiku form, it became my new favorite poem style. The majority of poems in this book are haiku. Words with hidden meanings come easily to me in this form and they are still my most frequently made poem.

I have never taken a formal class in poetry. My poems seem to write themselves. When I became more confident about my writing, I discovered giving poems to my family on special occasions captured a sentimental part of me (and my family). They enjoyed the sincerity of my words and I enjoyed giving them a piece of me. It encouraged my growth.

Along with the pleasure of putting words to paper, I was inspired to write this book because of my appreciation for the rich beauty and history of living in the quiet New England town of Guilford, CT. It is neither farm nor city, but quite interesting in it's simplicity. There are many beautiful places in Guilford that have sparked my interest over the years – most notably the shoreline of Sachem's Head, Indian Cove and Mulberry Point. I specifically admire the diversity of the many beautiful gates of Guilford. So, I decided to use the gates to illustrate my poems. Hopefully, it will give you a glimpse of what lies behind my words and offer new and exhilarating perpectives on what has been standing before us for so many years.

Lanzi W. Butler

Haiku

HAIKU is a popular form of Japanese poetry. Haiku poetry usually describes your feelings or reflects on nature. The modern haiku syntax consists of three lines of 5, 7 and 5 syllables that do not rhyme.

The haiku is my favorite form of poetry. Compact ideas coming together in a uniform haiku style come easily and I find it more interesting to create poems by syllables rather than rhyme.

Twin Statues

Stand like twin statues -
these sentries protect the walk
and embrace the light.

Black Flame

The black flame burns bright
     stairred against the white doorway -
        all are invited.

Cemetery

The gate-keeper lived
      in this old, cryptic manor -
            never to be seen.

Stripes

White stripes on red stripes
    paint patriotic visions -
        all over the town.

Flag

The British flag hides
  within the white garden gate -
    America lives.

UnFair

Strip of pearly whites
        defend us from the outside -
            are slightly open.

Welcome Sign

The garden within
            gives children a place to play -
                  fantasy of dreams.

The Stone Path

The stone path greets us
      the solitary tree guards -
            only the brave pass.

Old Country Farm

An old country farm
    bound by simple sticks and stones
        keep history in.

Ghostly Arm

Shadows cast upon –
      ghostly arm taunts all nature
            but holds careful watch.

Stones

The mixture of stones
        provides support all around
            for this festive gate.

Ballast

This historic stone -
        counterweight of a journey
            down the road of life.

Dim Door

Safely hid from man
     this dim door welcomes no one
        to the bright beyond.

Portrait

Standing wide open
    lies the portrait of a man
        captured in his gates.

Tanka

The TANKA poem is an extension of the modern day haiku. The syllabic pattern is 5, 7, 5, 7, 7, across five lines that do not rhyme. It originated from the ancient Japanese form of *renga*.

Tyrannosaur

Placed as an icon
The 'T' stands weighted alone
On the vacant sky.
Sun's radiant reflections
Criticize the dark keeper.

Piece of History

A strange formation
Stood for eras in Guilford
History has passed
The power of Freedom lives
Peace has kept it's foundation.

Gateway to Simplicity

Autumn leaves blowing
Embroidered along the mast
Frayed on all edges
Add tint to the phantom sky
Surrounding simplicity.

Acrostic

In ACROSTIC poetry the first letter of each line spells out the title of the poem. It is often used with children to initiate an interest in poetry. These poems are fun. They are easy to write and can have powerful meanings. An acrostic poem does not have to rhyme and is not bound by any number of syllables.

NEW ENGLAND

Nature unfolds behind these polls,
Explosive color consumes the scene,
Wilderness roams free.

Extravgant structure towers,
Never too old to appreciate the beauty,
Guiltless expansion
Lasting for centuries
Admired by folks both far and near,
Noble farmer survivies the ages,
Drenched in anonymity.

Monster

Mysterious trail leads to promise
Ominous Cerberus keeps vigil
No one dares to enter the
Smorgasbord of dreams.
Titanium custodian
Emerges from the myth and
Retreats to his sanctuary.

THE RIVER

The subdued charm of this gate
Haunts the River and
Ensnares my vision of the Stream.

Random bits of light and time
Inspire a new age.
Vacuous and
Empty, it liberates a
Renaissance of opinions.

Quatrain

A QUATRAIN is characterized by any amount of verses containing four lines (hence the prefix "quad-"). Quatrains have a specific rhyming scheme.

Some examples are:
- lines ending in a,b,a,b
- lines ending in a,b,b,a
- lines ending in a,a,b,b

Blinding Light

Clouds divide the heavenly sky,
Peers through the pitckets, a sliver of light,
Divine diffusion scars the eye,
And captures a dream abandoned by sight.

Gargoyle

Garbled and mean, you resign your fate
To guard this province from all who hate,
Caged within, your ire appears,
Imprisoned by time and riddled with fears.

Echoes of laughter, heighten your power,
Adds to the rage that makes you sour,
Fuels your aggression by light of day
And gives you strength in every way.

Feeling comfort in the shadow,
Darkness, your friend, not your foe,
Sinister beginnings and shrouded in mystery,
Reassuring obscurity is your history.

Z

Trapped within a Z-ish spell,
A life concealed and hidden well,
Tragic secrets twist truth and trust,
Becomes the norm for pride and lust.

Tyburn

A TYBURN poem consists of six lines with an unusual syllabic arrangement of 2, 2, 2, 2, 9, 9.

The first four bisyllabic lines must rhyme and they should descibe the title. The fifth line rhymes and includes the words used in the first two lines. The sixth line also rhymes and includes the third and fourth descriptive lines.

Long Reflections

Greetful,
Peaceful,
Tranquil,
Wistful,
Contrast the greetful, peaceful forest,
Inspires a tranquil, wistful thought.

Fenceless

Mindless,
Hopeless,
Helpless,
Fenceless,
Stuck in the mindless, hopeless muddle,
Reclines the helpless, fenceless timber.

Hidden Hideaway

Greener,
Meaner,
Darker,
Smarter,
Misplaced in a greener, meaner lawn,
There appeared a darker, smarter way.

Cinquain

The CINQUAIN was developed in 1909 by the poet Adelaide Crapsy who was influenced by the Japanese Haiku.

A cinquain is a short poem consisting of twenty-two syllables across five lines in an arranged pattern of 2, 4, 6, 8, 2 that do not rhyme.

Arrows

Arrows,
All parallel,
Piercing a wall of sky,
Silhouette cast upon the trees,
Iron pikes.

Profile Corral

Profile
Dark upon light
It protects and forgives
Unstable and weak, it preserves
Corral

Trellis

Trellis
Looking over,
Companion to the tree,
Creates a feeling of armor,
Catwalk.

Lanturne

LANTURNES are short poems consisting of five lines with the syllabic pattern of 1, 2, 3, 4, 1. This particular pattern gives the poems the physical shape of a Japanese lantern.

Silhouette

Curl
Spiraled
Coil formed curve
Twisted and scrolled
Grows.

Pool

Pool
Empty
Childhood dreams
Magical play
Swim!

Red Path

Red
flowing
on the path
upstream or down,
clash.

Naani

A NAANI is another short poem of four lines. Each line is not bound to a particular subject or by syllabic restrictions but the stanza has a total of 20 - 25 syllables.

Naani means an expression of one and all. This form of poetry was introduced by Telugu poet, Dr. N. Gopi. It is one of India's most popular styles.

Description courtesy of ShadowPoetry.com.

Arched Ramble

Creeping vine of leaves,
Inching along the arched ramble,
Grazes my head,
Makes me feel humble.

Yellow Sky

Autumn silence
Yellow sky
Checkered gate
Inspires me to contemplate.

Primitive Sculpture

Primitive sculpture
Hidden in the jungle
Lures the innocent to the darkness
And captures the light.

Diamante

A DIAMANTE poem is a seven line poem. The text takes the shape of a diamond.

The set-up of the poem is:

Line 1:   One word (noun).
Line 2:   Two adjectives describe the first word.
Line 3:   Three '-ing' words describe the first word
Line 4:   First two words connect with the first word;
          the last two words connect with the last word.
Line 5:   Three '-ing' words describe the last word.
Line 6:   Two adjectives describe the last word.
Line 7:   One word (noun) as a synonym or antonym of
          the first word.

Holiday

Holiday
cheerful, sociable,
caroling, wrapping, visiting
festival, garland, birthday, lights
dancing, eating, blessing,
joyful, gregarious
Celebration!

Lock

Lock
protected, fortified
restraining, containing, blockading
repressor, controller, unveiler, wedge
aligning, turning, opening,
metallic, trustworthy
Key.

Bell

Bell,
ancient, resonant,
ringing, dangling, oxidizing
symbol, gesture, noise, echo
clanging, sounding, harmonizing,
brilliant, silent,
Chime.

Shape

Like acrostic poetry, SHAPE poetry shares a visual link with the title of the poem. In shape poems a feeling is often enhanced by shaping the words in the poem like something relating to the subject.

Guilford Scenery

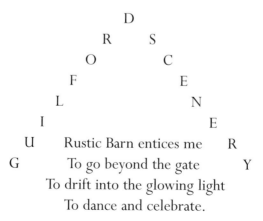

```
            D
        R       S
      O           C
      F             E
    L                 N
  I                     E
U        Rustic Barn entices me    R
G          To go beyond the gate      Y
          To drift into the glowing light
            To dance and celebrate.
```

"Meautiful" Splendor

An open field is interrupted with a line of "meautiful" splendor.

The Heart

A trivial   heart
e m b e d d e d   w i t h i n
appears too shallow for true love to begin.
Behind these walls and determined by love
are shattered remains or high flying doves.
If choosing desire, a risk you will take,
make   the   wrong   move,
the   h e a r t   you
m i g h t
break

!

Color

In a COLOR poem sensations are described by the poet using prominent colors through literary similies and other comparisons. Color poems have no syllabic, rhythmic or length restrictions. A color poem can stretch forever if the author has much to describe.

A popular way to describe those feelings of color is through the five senses:

> looks like…
> sounds like…
> smells like…
> tastes like…
> feels like…

Yellow

Yellow is the feeling of the sun warming your face,
Yellow is the sound of 'deja vu',
Yellow is the smell of pine at the tree lighting,
Yellow is the taste of banana daiquiris in Atlantis,
Yellow is the look of a familiar landmark.

White

White looks like a sprawling descending staircase,
White sounds like decrescendoing piano keys,
White smells like oyster shells stacked in a
      mountain of glory,
White tastes like cold pasteurized milk,
White feels like powdery snow on a chilled
      winter morning.

Red

Red is a color that forbids me to pass.
Red is the sight of weathering clapboards on this
      colonial house.
Red is the feeling of Christmas on a cold winter day.
Red is the smell of sizzling rare cooked barbecue.
Red is the sound of howling neighborhood dogs.
Red is the taste of crisp Empire apples on a chilled fall
      picnic.

Epitaph

An EPITAPH or an *ode* is very similar to a quatrain in that it has a specific rhyming scheme. However, there is no requirement of lines per stanza or stanzas per verse.

The majority of the poem praises the subject without digressing. Epitaphs are used as inscriptions on tombstones in the memory of the person buried.

Ode to a Broken Gate

Tall and structured, this gate once stood,
Mounted with metal and not just wood,
That angry soul, your beauty they took,
Is not concerned of how you look.

Fractured and lame, I feel your pain,
For the crippled life you now maintain,
Your dismantled appearance you can't conceal,
Surely in time your wounds shall heal.

Ode to a Giant

While driving one day, the road did end,
I came across a giant friend,
Stood tall and black, strong message to send,
The stones, the foliage, all seemed to blend.

I marveled at length, its perplexing stature,
Tiles and rocks, cement its architecture,
Clearly made for one of royalty,
'Tis a gate that lacks genuine subtlety.

Hanging

Hanging still upon the door
A trail of leaves fall to the floor
The path of bricks we must ignore
To save the image forevermore.

About the Author

Lanzi W. Butler has born in 1988 and he has lived his entire life in the town of Guilford, CT. Much of his free time is spent playing or practicing music. At times you can hear the sound of Lanzi's trumpet drifting through the trees along the shoreline at midnight or ringing from the rooftop of his house at dusk. In addition to these random neighborhood concerts, Lanzi plays with the Guilford High School *Wind Ensemble* and the *Jazz Band*. Among his other musical accomplishments, he was accepted to perform in the *2005 Connecticut Regional and All-State Jazz Ensemble*. He has also played with the *Connecticut Youth Jazz Band*.

As a member of the *Sports Band*, Lanzi is a dedicated *BFL* football player on Fridays. He also enjoys an occasional game of *Mafia* with his Debate Team buddies. Aside from having fun with his dog Cooper, Lanzi has always enjoyed working with kids. He tutors seventh and eight graders in math during the school year and he is a camp counselor at Deer Lake in the summer.

Music may be his passion, but poetry has launched Lanzi's appreciation for the humanities. Whatever he creates - be it poetry or music - is truly a treasure.